MW01381121

First published 2004 by Moondrake
a division of Harcourt Education Australia.
18–22 Salmon Street, Port Melbourne, Victoria, 3207 Australia
(a division of Reed International Books Australia Pty Ltd, ABN 70 001 002 357)

℞ A Reed Elsevier company

Cover picture selection by Paul and Faye Wyer
Photographs © Ken Stepnell 2004
© Murray David Publishing 2004
Design © Murray David Publishing 2004
Printed in Indonesia

First published 2004

ISBN: 1 74070209 3

10 9 8 7 6 5 4 3 2 1

All rights reserved. No part of this publication
may be reproduced, stored in a retrieval system, or transmitted in any form
or by any means, (electronic, mechanical, photocopying, recording or
otherwise) without the prior permission of the Publisher.

AUSTRALIA

Photography by Ken Stepnell
Text by Dalys Newman

From Reno & Margaret Vassallo
February 2007

MOONDRAKE

PRECEDING PAGE: Canberra panorama, seen from the lookout on the summit of Mount Ainslie.

ABOVE: The heart of the nation—Parliament House on Capitol Hill. Designed by Aldo Giurgola, and costing nearly $1billion, it was officially opened in 1988. Its magnificent 81 metre stainless steel flagpole dominates Canberra's skyline.

BELOW LEFT: The telecommunication tower on the summit of Black Mountain stands sentinel over the tranquil waters of Lake Burley Griffin.

BELOW RIGHT: Canberra, Australia's national capital, is one of the world's best known fully planned cities. Designed by Walter Burley Griffin, the city boasts impressive public buildings, parkland and bush reserves, leafy suburbs and broad tree-lined streets.

OPPOSITE: The Captain Cook Memorial Jet, shooting a 137 metre column of water into the air, and the terrestrial globe showing Cook's voyages of discovery are decorative features of Lake Burley Griffin, Canberra.

4   AUSTRALIA

OPPOSITE: Forever inseparable, the Three Sisters stand sentinel over the spectacular scenery of the Blue Mountains National Park. Once part of the cliff at Echo Point, these famous pinnacles of rock were left standing when the cliff was undermined, great blocks of it falling away into the valley.

ABOVE: Sydney's CBD, seen from Mrs Macquaries Point. From a humble and adventurous beginning in 1788, Sydney has grown into Australia's largest and most exciting city.

CENTRE: The Opera House, one of Sydney's best known icons, makes a dramatic statement on the city foreshore. The sculpted masterpiece is sited on Bennelong Point, adjacent to Circular Quay, on a priceless finger of land jutting into the harbour. Designed by Danish architect, Joern Utzon, and costing $102 million, it was officially opened in 1973.

RIGHT: Bondi Beach in Sydney is Australia's most famous stretch of surf, sand and sunshine. It is one of the 34 beaches that the city has to offer.

ABOVE: Coffs Harbour in New South Wales is home to a modern fishing fleet. The coastal resort town, famous for its bananas and fishing, is a popular base for adventure seekers.

ABOVE RIGHT: The Warrumbungles form an eerie landscape of jagged cliffs, rocky pinnacles and crags jutting out from the western slopes of the Great Dividing Range near Coonabarabran in New South Wales. This ancient mountain range, the remnants of a volcano, was named after the Aboriginal word for 'crooked mountains'.

RIGHT: The Snowy Mountain region covers a wide area of the highest mountain ranges in Australia, stretching through New South Wales and Victoria. Here are found the country's finest ski fields and Mt Kosciusko, Australia's highest peak.

OPPOSITE: The two-tier Ebor Falls in the New England National Park, New South Wales, mark the place where the Guy Fawkes River takes its first spectacular plunge off the Northern Tablelands.

OVERLEAF: Sydney Harbour Bridge is the world's largest steel arch bridge and, with its 49 metre wide deck, the widest longspan bridge in the world. Its total length, including approach spans, is 1149 metres and its arch span is 503 metres.

ABOVE: The luxurious resort destination of Hamilton Island, in the Whitsundays, is one of 74 tropical islands that lie between the Queensland coast and the Great Barrier Reef.

ABOVE RIGHT: A charming blend of old and new, Townsville is a relaxed coastal city renowned for its magnificent tropical climate. The capital of north Queensland, it is the main administrative, commercial and manufacturing city in the region. Remnants of early settlement are evident in the colonial architecture, historic pubs, museums and displays of goldmining machinery.

CENTRE RIGHT: Picking pineapples near Budrem, Queensland. Pineapples were introduced to Queensland, probably from India, around 1838. They are now widely cultivated in the narrow coastal strip along the eastern seaboard, from Cairns in the north to Brisbane in the south.

RIGHT: City meets the sea at Surfers Paradise, Queensland. The Gold Coast area, with its high-rise hotels, casinos and seemingly endless stretches of sand, attracts over 3 million tourists from around the world each year.

LEFT: Brisbane, the capital of Queensland, is Australia's third largest city and busiest river port. Relaxed and easygoing, the city was named after the Governor of New South Wales, Sir Thomas Brisbane. Straddling the Brisbane River, and sprawling over a small series of hills, it is filled with lush parks and gardens brimming with tropical plants.

BELOW: Gradual weathering by wind and rain has produced the Glasshouse Mountains, spectacular remains of volcanic activity more than 20 million years ago. Creating a surreal landscape north of Brisbane, these mountains were named by Captain James Cook who thought they resembled glass foundries near his home in Yorkshire. More importantly, they stand as a timeless reminder of the Kabi Aborigines, for whom they had great Dreamtime significance. A total of fifteen mountains ranging from 100 to 556 metres cover an area of 600 000 hectares.

OPPOSITE: Plunging 109 metres into a mist-shrouded abyss, Purlingbrook Falls, on the Gold Coast, are spectacular after heavy rainfalls.

RIGHT: In the heart of the reef and rainforest coast, picturesque Port Douglas has become an international holiday mecca with its sweeping Four Mile Beach, its tropical old world charm and array of world class restaurants and accommodation.

BELOW: Shute Harbour, Queensland, launching pad for exploring the hundred or so tropical islands of the beautiful Whitsunday waters. This tiny settlement is effectively nothing more than a lot of parking spaces and a harbour from which ferries and cruise boats depart.

BELOW RIGHT: Todd Mall, in the central business district of Alice Springs, offers shade from the unrelenting sun of the Red Centre. The second largest town in the Northern Territory, 'The Alice', as it is affectionately known, was once a vital link on the Overland Telegraph Line and is now a popular destination for tourists exploring the nearby MacDonnell Ranges, Uluru and Kata Tjuta.

BOTTOM RIGHT: Australia's only beachside hotel casino, MGM Grand Darwin is surrounded by lush tropical gardens. On the shores of Mindil Beach, this casino has over 370 slot machines and a gaming room.

OPPOSITE: Steep and stark, the 5 metre wide walls of Standley Chasm, a spectacular cleft in the MacDonnell Ranges, west of Alice Springs. The craggy walls rise 80 metres above the floor and the chasm is so narrow that light only reaches the base about midday when the walls glow from reflected sunlight.

ABOVE: The weathered rounded boulders of the Devil's Marbles balance precariously on top of one another beside the highway to Alice Springs, south of Tennant Creek. In Aboriginal mythology, these stones were said to be the eggs of the Rainbow Serpent.

BELOW: Edith Falls tumble into a natural pool fringed with paperbarks and pandanus. This idyllic spot on the western boundary of the Nitmiluk National Park, near Katherine, is popular with campers and bushwalkers.

ABOVE: Ellery Gorge with its spectacular cliff faces and cool waterhole is one of many gorges found in the Alice Springs region of Central Australia. Ellery Creek is the main tributary of the Finke River and joins it in the middle of the Krichauff Range.

CENTRE: One of the most prominent gaps in the West MacDonnell Ranges in the Northern Territory, Simpsons Gap was named by Surveyor McMinn in 1871 while he was exploring possible routes for the Overland Telegraph Line. At dawn or dusk black-footed rock wallabies can commonly be seen hopping along the short walking track into the Gap.

LEFT: The rich colours of Glen Helen Gorge, on the Finke River west of Alice Springs have been immortalised in the paintings of Aboriginal artist Albert Namatjira.

OPPOSITE: The Katherine River flows below the towering, brilliantly coloured walls of Katherine Gorge in Nitmiluk National Park.

LEFT: Estimated to be 2700 million years old, the remarkable 15 metre high Wave Rock is near Hyden in Western Australia. A 110 metre long granite cliff, its rounded shape has been caused by weathering and water erosion which has undercut the base and left a rounded overhang. Water running down the rock has dissolved minerals, creating the colourful effect.

BELOW: Strange rock formations are a feature of King's Canyon in Watarka National Park. Notable for the severity of its rock formations, the canyon is bordered by ancient sandstone walls rising 100 metres to a plateau of rocky domes and is the Red Centre's deepest and most striking gorge.

ABOVE LEFT: The rugged peaks of the Stirling Ranges rise abruptly out of countryside rich in native vegetation. Preserved since early this century the whole Stirling Range has escaped the impact of settlement and is a haven for a large variety of flowering plants.

CENTRE LEFT: Rock formations at Marble Bar in outback Western Australia. Named after a local deposit of mineral first thought to be marble, but later proved to be jasper, this mining centre is reputedly the hottest town in Australia.

ABOVE: Situated on the banks of the Swan River, Perth, the capital of Western Australia was first settled in 1829. Australia's sunniest capital, it averages 7.8 hours of sunshine per day.

LEFT: One of Western Australia's most popular tourist attractions, Burswood Casino is nestled on the banks of the Swan River in Perth. Costing $650 million, the international resort casino complex opened in 1988 and was an important milestone for the State's developing hospitality and tourism industry.

TOP LEFT: Sidewalk cafes are a major attraction at the charming port city of Fremantle in Western Australia. Known as the 'Gateway to the West', this bustling city was first settled in 1829 and was the first colony in Australia made up entirely of free settlers. Beautiful old colonial buildings dating back to the early 1830s and sandy white beaches make it a vibrant tourist precinct.

LEFT: One of the wonders of outback Australia, the Bungle Bungles in Purnululu National Park are sandstone towers formed over 350 million years ago. The range, with its distinctive beehive-shaped rock formations, rises up to 578 metres above sea level, standing 200 to 300 metres above a woodland and grass-covered plain.

LEFT: Hawks Head lookout affords magnificent views over the wild landscape of Kalbarri National Park, encompassing the lower reaches of the Murchison River. This mighty 800 kilometre river has carved deep gorges and winding valleys out of the coastal sandstone and after heavy rains is a muddy brown torrent.

LEFT: Granite cliffs and headlands combined with peaceful sandy bays create dramatic coastal scenery in the Cape Le Grand National Park in Western Australia. The 31 390 hectare park is named after Le Grand, an officer of the *L'Esperance,* one of the ships in a French expedition commanded by Admiral D'Entrecasteaux in 1792.

OPPOSITE: An unbroken wall of cliffs borders the Nullarbor Plain on the Great Australian Bight, stretching all the way to the tip of the Eyre Peninsula, where it reaches an imposing end in the Lincoln National Park.

OPPOSITE: The old and the new—the modern Victoria Square fountain contrasts with the historic Adelaide Town Hall. Named after King William IV's queen, Adelaide is a gracious well-planned city. The South Australian capital, it is home to more than one million people.

TOP RIGHT: The spacious city of Adelaide is situated on the Torrens River on a narrow coastal plain between the blue waters of Gulf St Vincent and the rolling hills of the Mt Lofty Ranges. The stream-lined, modern Festival Centre, on the banks of the river, is home of the biennial Festival of Arts.

RIGHT: The white sands of Glenelg, Adelaide's most popular beach. Only a short drive from the centre of Adelaide, it can also be reached by a vintage tram which departs from Victoria Square. Grand old homes and guesthouses along the foreshore are a reminder of the town's days as an exclusive seaside resort.

RIGHT: Christmas Cove provides a small, safe anchorage for the fishing boats at Penneshaw on Kangaroo Island, 14.5 kilometres off the coast of South Australia. Here, nature is seen at its best with a magical combination of sun, sea, native flora and fauna.

BOTTOM RIGHT: A unique feature on the west coast of South Australia, Murphy's Haystacks are fine examples of weathered pink granite inselberg structures. Over 34 000 years old, these finely sculpted forms are often encrusted with lichen growths.

OVERLEAF: The Remarkable Rocks, a group of huge granite boulders, created by the rough swells and strong winds rolling in from the Southern Ocean, are features of the wild and majestic Flinders Chase National Park on Kangaroo Island. This park comprises almost the entire western part of the island and is an area rich in natural features and native animals entirely at ease with their human visitors.

ABOVE: Melbourne, on the banks of the Yarra River, is Australia's second largest city and the capital of Victoria. With a population of more than 3 million, it is regarded as the cultural and fashion capital of Australia and renowned for its fine restaurants. A true multicultural city, one quarter of Melbourne's inhabitants were born overseas.

BELOW LEFT: Southbank, stretching along the southern bank of the Yarra River, was once an old industrial area and has been rejuvenated as the heartbeat of the central city area. The main focal point is the Southgate Arts and Leisure Precinct which is Melbourne's main entertainment area.

BELOW RIGHT: Skiers enjoy the snow fields at Falls Creek, the premier skiing resort in the Victorian Alps.

OPPOSITE: Triplet Falls, tumbling in three stages through rainforest bushland, are one of the many waterfalls found in the steep slopes and tall forests of the Otway Ranges which merge with the Southern Ocean to form a 12 876 hectare national park in Victoria.

OPPOSITE: The Twelve Apostles, renowned natural sculptures formed by seas pounding the limestone plateau around Port Campbell on Victoria's south coast.

ABOVE: The Balconies (previously known as the Jaws of Death) provide an excellent vantage point for the intrepid sightseer in the Grampians National Park, Victoria. Declared in 1984, the 167 000 hectare park is renowned for its rugged mountain ranges and stunning wildflower displays. It is home for almost a third of Victoria's plant species.

CENTRE RIGHT: Autumn tones reflect in the dam waters at Mt Beauty, high up in the Kiewa Valley. Tucked beneath Mt Bogong, the highest peak in the Victorian Alps, this alpine town is set amongst rich valleys, snow-clad mountains, lakes and wild rivers.

BOTTOM RIGHT: Towering above the Ovens Valley, the high granite plateau of Mount Buffalo National Park looks out over the spectacular peaks of the Victorian Alps with the Razorback Range in the distance.

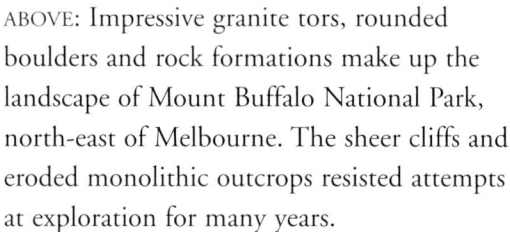

ABOVE: Impressive granite tors, rounded boulders and rock formations make up the landscape of Mount Buffalo National Park, north-east of Melbourne. The sheer cliffs and eroded monolithic outcrops resisted attempts at exploration for many years.

CENTRE LEFT: Hobart, seen from Montagu Bay, was Australia's second European settlement. Established in 1804, it is memorable for its deep-water harbour on the estuary of the Derwent River, its mellow early colonial sandstone buildings and the backdrop of majestic Mt Wellington.

BOTTOM LEFT: Richmond Bridge, spanning the Coal River in Tasmania, is Australia's oldest bridge. It was built by convicts between 1823 and 1825 and is said to be haunted by their cruel overseer.

OPPOSITE: Liffy Falls, near Deloraine in Tasmania, are a spectacular example of the many beautiful waterfalls found in the rainforests of this State. Many fern species grow around the waterways in these rainforests and as the terrain rises, communities of myrtle beech, sassafrass, native laurel and celery-top pine are found.

LEFT: Unloading abalone at Constitution Dock, Hobart. Abalone form the basis of one of Tasmania's most important domestic and export industries, producing 2607.5 tonnes annually, 25% of global production. In this busy dock area it is possible to dine at a seafood restaurant or purchase fresh seafood from local fishermen. After Christmas every year, the dock is evacuated to make room for participants in the Sydney to Hobart yacht race, one of the finest blue-water ocean classics in the world.

BELOW: Hiking is a popular activity near Dove Lake in the Cradle Mountain–Lake St Clair National Park, Tasmania. This area has dense forests of deciduous beech, Tasmanian myrtle, pencil and King Billy pine with an undergrowth of mosses and ferns. Tasmania's most famous park, it encompasses an area of 131 915 hectares.

INDEX